IPv4   IPv6 Technology and Implementation

Internet protocol version 4 / version6 Technology and Implementation

Written by Ghazi Mokammel Hossain

The book consists of brief discussion about the Internet Protocol IPv4 / IPv6 technology and implementations of the technology

Acknowledgement

Internet has greater contribution towards modern civilization. Next generation will share this contribution of technological knowledge. Internet protocol is the necessary things for computer networking. Computer networking totally depends on this protocol. In this book I have written about total descriptions of Internet Protocol version 4 and 6. I have also shown the relations, advantages, disadvantages between Ipv4 and 6 and the difference between these two technologies. I have also shown the implementations of these technologies by analyzing the technology, network designing and testing the some part of this technology. With the help and cooperation of my university Computer Science Engineering department teacher, my father, mother and my cousin I have completed the project. I am great full to them. I hope my book will be helpful towards advance knowledge of IPv4/ IPv6 technologies and the implementation of the technology.

Details of the book

Written by: Ghazi Mokammel Hossain

Editing and Proofread by: G.M Hossain
Ghazi Mozammel Hossain

Cover Page Design by: Ghazi Mokammel Hossain

Date of Publication: 2 November 2013

Publications Format: Amazon Kindle Digital E-Book format, Amazon CreateSpace Hard copy format

Edition No: First Edition

Publication From: Dhaka, Bangladesh

Version: International Version

Published by: Amazon Kindle Direct Publishing

ISBN-13: 978-1493696444

ISBN-10: 1493696440   (The book has been assigned a CreateSpace ISBN)

Publication Language type: English

Email address: gmjon21@gmail.com

Skype Id: gmhossain380
Phone no: +8801674950802

Copyright

Dedicated To

* *
* *

I dedicate this book to my beloved father and mother

* *
* *
* * *

Table of Content

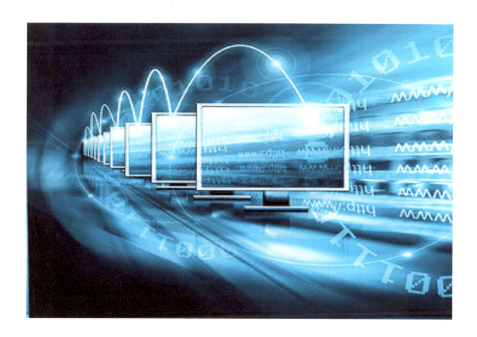

Chapter 1: Introduction

1.1 What is Internet Protocol?

Internet protocol (IP) is the protocol or method by which information is sent from one pc to another on the Online or Internet. Each pc (known as a host) on the Online has at least one IP address with that exclusively identifies it from all other computer on the Internet.

When you deliver or get information (for example, an e-mail observe or a Web page), the concept gets separated into little sections known as packet. Each of these packets contains both the sender's internet address with and the receiver's address. Any packet is sent first to a gateway pc that is aware of a small sector of the Online. The gateway pc flows the location deal with and sends the packet to an nearby gateway that in turn flows the location address and so forth across the Online until one gateway identifies the packet as that belong to a pc within its immediate community or sector. That gateway then sends the packet straight to the pc whose address is specified.

Because a concept is separated into a number of packets, each packet can, if necessary, be sent by a different path across the Online. Packets can appear in a different order than the transaction they were sent in. The IP just provides them. It's up to another protocol, the Transmitting Control Protocol (TCP) to put them back in the right order.

IP is a connectionless protocol, which means that there is no ongoing relationship between the end factors that are interacting. Each packet that moves through the Online is handled as a separate device of information without any regards to any other device of information. (The reason the packages do get put in the right order because of TCP, the connection-oriented protocol that keeps a record of the packet series in a concept.) In the Open Systems Interconnection (OSI) communication design, IP is in layer 3, the network Layer.

The most commonly used edition of IP these days is Internet Protocol version 4 (IPv4). However, IP Version 6 (IPv6) is also starting to be reinforced. IPv6 provides for much more addresses and therefore for the likelihood of many more Online surfers. IPv6 contains the abilities of IPv4 and any servers that can assistance IPv6 packets can also assistance IPv4 packets.

There are five types of Internet Protocol:

1. Hyper text transfer protocol: Hyper Text Transfer Protocol, the actual protocol used by the World Wide Web. HTTP describes how information are arranged and passed on, and what actions Web servers and internet explorer should take in reaction to various instructions. For example, when you enter a URL in your web browser, this actually delivers an HTTP control to the Web server guiding it to bring and transfer the asked for Web page.

2. Fiber Channel network protocols: Fiber Channel Protocol (FCP) is the standard transportation protocol for providing sequential SCSI instructions over Fiber Route interconnects. Fiber Channel Protocol is designed to function in a highly-efficient way using hardware for protocol offload engines (POEs). Such highly-integrated POEs were necessary for the high-performance requirements of customers who implemented Fiber channel at first as a fast, effective, scalable data transportation system and later, to allow and build Storage Area System (SAN) set ups. Fiber Route Method standardization is the liability of the INCITS TC-T10 panel.

3. Internet Protocol Suite or TCP/IP model or TCP/IP stacks: TCP/IP (transmission control protocol/Internet protocol) is the package of communication protocol that is used to link serves on the Online and on most other laptop or computer systems as well. It is also generally known as the TCP/IP protocol and the IP address protocol suite.

A method is a mutually agreed-upon structure for doing something. With respect to laptop or computer systems, it most generally relates a set of guidelines (i.e., a standard) that allows laptop or computer systems to link and transfer information to one another; this is also known as a communications protocol.

4. OSI protocols: Open Systems Interconnection protocol family of information exchange standards jointly developed by the ISO and the ITU-T in 1977. OSI protocol stacks are divided into seven layers. The layers form a structure of performance beginning with the physical elements components to the user interface at the software program level. Each part gets detail information from the layer above, procedures it and goes it down to the next layer. Each layer contributes its own encapsulation information (header) to the inbound information before it is approved to the lower layer. Headers generally consist of deal with of location and resource, check amounts (for mistake control), type of method used in the current part, and other choices such as circulation management choices and series figures (used to make sure information is sent in order).

5. Yahoo! Messenger Protocol (YMSG): An underlying protocol used by the Yahoo messenger
Yahoo! messenger instant messaging, for Yahoo! Yahoo! Immediate Messenger facilitates many features beyond just texting, such as off-line texting, computer file exchange, talk, conference meetings, speech talk, webcams and virtual representations of personnel.
The objective of the YMSG method is to provide a language and sequence of conferences for software interacting with Yahoo!'s Immediate Messaging support. Essentially YMSG works the same part for IM as HTTP does for the World Wide Web. Compared with HTTP, however, YMSG is an exclusive standard, arranged only with a single texting support agency (namely, Yahoo!). Competing texting services have their own methods, some based on open standards, others exclusive, each successfully satisfying the same part with different techniques.

6. Real-Time Publish-Subscribe (RTPS) Wire Protocol: RTPS is an interoperability protocol used to allow multi-vendor Data Distribution Service Support (DDS) implementations to communicate. The Real-Time Publish-Subscribe (RTPS) method is developed for use with Internet Protocol (IP) one-to-many Multicast and connectionless best-effort carries such as IP User Datagram Protocol (UDP).

The main features of the RTPS protocol include:

*Performance and Quality-of-Service (QoS) properties: allowing best-effort and reliable publish-subscribe communication for real-time programs using standard IP network.
*Fault tolerance: Allowing the creation of systems without single points of failing.
*Extensibility: Allowing in reverse interface and interoperability through additions of the method and improvement with new solutions.
*Plug-and-play: Connection for new programs and solutions allowing automatic, configuration-less finding by programs becoming a member of and leaving the system whenever they want.
*Configurability: Allowing controlling the requirements of stability and timeliness for each data delivery deal.
*Modularity: Allowing simple devices to apply a part of the method and still get involved in the publish-subscribe system.
*Scalability: Allowing systems to scale to very large publish-subscribe systems.
*Type-safety: Avoiding application development mistakes limiting the operation of remote   nodes in the publish-subscribe system.

1.2 Abstraction of the Industry:

Before execution of IPv4, technicians and researchers operating on ARPANET discussed on the duration of an IP address. The discussion was between 32-bit and 128-bit deal with measures. Although the agreement was 128-bit, Vint Cerf, in 1977, determined to use a 32-bit duration for the IPv4 deal with. He created this choice because he never foresaw the need for more than 4.3 billion dollars deal with and desired to shift the venture ahead. Thus, IPv4 was to be 32-bits lengthy and the World Wide Web was created. On the 3rd of Feb 2011, the Online Organization for Allocated Titles and Figures (ICANN) passed out the last prevent of the IPv4 addresses.

The causing deficiency of IPv4 address prevents leads to constant fall of IPv4 address space. To save and recycling the deal with prevents, companies (SP) resort to systems like multiple levels of Network Address Translation (NAT). The more ideal approach to fix the issue of address deficiency experiencing the social networking industry is to move towards the IPv6 addressing with plan. IPv6 provides 3.4×10^{38} addresses and comes with other additional developments. First, it provides improved performance in redirecting. Second, it provides quicker bundle handling. Third, it facilitates multicast thereby overwhelming the complications of transmitting packages. 4th, it prevents system deal with interpretation (NAT), therefore, shows to be more robust.

IPv6 adopting has been slowly and encounters several challenges. First, there is no true financial owner for organizations. The fatigue of IPv4 deal with space has been promoted for decades and the market has designed technological innovation to boost IPv4 deal with utilization. The most popular of these technological innovations is Network Address Translation (NAT). NAT assisted to force out the fatigue of IPv6 by roughly a several years. This has purchased time for IPv6 to older further. During this season's world IPv6 day, the objective is to allow roughly one percent of the Internet with IPv6 assistance. This is not a calculate of real IPv6 traffics. The professionals anticipate IPv6 traffics to improve significantly in the future.

1.3 Research:

The need of the time is to allow IPv6 abilities on all current systems. However, IPv4 systems cannot update to IPv6 systems instantly. This is partly due to the understanding of the specialized immaturity of IPv6 as in comparison to IPv4. Also, companies are extremely risk-adverse and are not responsive to new changes so instantly. Furthermore, there is a deficiency of IPv6 attention. The specialized incompatibilities to turn all the system gadgets to comprehend IPv6 instantly are another problem that must be met. These aspects cause us to look for solutions that assistance co-existence of IPv4 and IPv6 dealing with techniques in networks. This project document provides a wide opportunity of IPv4/IPv6 co-existence technology perfect for a company network system. There are several options for further analysis. The circumstances that were not mentioned are areas that require further analysis. In particular further analysis on technology that allows IPv4 hosts to connect with IPv6 hosts and network services is needed. Furthermore, each of the suggested technology could also be further investigated by discovering performance and execution problems.

So this project focuses on the implementation on Ipv4 and Ipv6 technology. It also shows the detail analysis result on the Ipv4 and Ipv6 technology.

Chapter 2: Literature Review

2.1 Review of the Research:

In the review of the research part we can say that IPv6 is upgrade form of theIPv4 .As IPv6 is a the upgrade form of the IPv4 it is more secured and faster than IPv4 .At the same time it contain huge networking data then IPv4.But the two systems are very much important for computer networking. These systems are design for developing the faster and secured computer networking system.

2.2 Ipv4 and Ipv6 Technology:

The detail of IPv4 technology is given below:

Internet Protocol version 4 (IPv4) is it all modification in the growth of the Internet Protocol (IP) and the first edition of the protocol to be commonly implemented. Together with IPv6, it is at the primary of standards-based internetworking techniques of the Online. As of 2012 IPv4 is still the most commonly implemented Online Part protocol.

IPv4 is described in IETF book RFC 791 (September 1981), changing a previously meaning (RFC 760, Jan 1980).

IPv4 is a connectionless protocol for use on packet-switched Web link Part systems (e.g., Ethernet). It functions on a best attempt distribution design, in that it does not assurance distribution, nor does it assurance appropriate sequencing or prevention of copy distribution. These factors, such as information reliability, are resolved by a higher layer transportation protocol, such as the Transmitting Management Method (TCP).

IPv4 uses 32-bit (four-byte) details, which boundaries the deal with area to 4294967296 addresses.

The advantages and disadvantages of IPv4 are as follows:

Advantages:

*Auto-configuration - Customers using IPv4 address use the Dynamic Host Configuration Protocol (DHCP) server every time they log onto a network system. This process is known as 'stateful auto-configuration.' IPv6 facilitates an improved DHCPv6 protocol to back up similar stateful auto-configuration, but also facilitates stateless auto-configuration of nodes that do not require a server to acquire details, but uses router ads to make a deal with. This makes a "plug-and-play" atmosphere and can make simpler control and administration.
* Commonly supported
*Shorter the sweeter (header)
*Support of All OS
*All Widely used methods are reinforced
*IPv6 tunnel over IPv4

Disadvantages:
* Restricted address area the most noticeable and immediate problem with using IPv4 on the modern Online is the fast destruction of community addresses. Due to the preliminary deal with category allowance methods of the beginning online, community IPv4 addresses are becoming limited. Companies in the U. S. Declares hold most community IPv4 deal with area globally.
* This limited address area has pressured the wide implementation of network address translators (NATs), which can discuss one community IPv4, address with among several independently resolved computer network systems. NATs have the complication of performing as a hurdle for server, audience, and peer-to-peer programs running on computer systems that are situated behind the NAT. Although there are workarounds for NAT problems, they only add complexness to what should be an end-to-end addressable international network system.

* Smooth redirecting facilities in the beginning Online, address with prefixes were not allocated to create a summarize able, ordered redirecting facilities. Instead, individual address prefixes were allocated and each address with prefix became a new path in the redirecting platforms of the online central source routers. Modern Online is an assortment of flat and ordered redirecting, but there are still more than 85,000 routers in the redirecting platforms of online central source routers.

* Settings IPv4 must be designed, either personally or through the Dynamic Host Configuration Protocol (DHCP). DHCP allows IPv4 configuration management to range to large systems, but you must also set up and handle DHCP facilities.

* Flexibility Mobility is a new need for Internet-connected gadgets, in which a node can change its address with as it changes its physical connection to the Online and still sustain current relationships. Although there is a requirements for IPv4 mobility, due to a lack of facilities, communication with an IPv4 mobile node are ineffective.

* Prioritized distribution Prioritized bundle distribution, such as special managing factors for low wait and low difference in wait for speech or video hosts, is possible with IPv4. However, it depends on a new presentation of the IPv4 Type of Service (TOS) area, which is not reinforced for all the gadgets on the network system. Additionally, recognition of the bundle circulation must be done using a higher part protocol identifier such as a TCP or Customer Datagram Method (UDP) slot. This additional managing of the bundle by advanced routers makes sending less effective.

The detail of IPv6 technology is given below:
Internet Protocol version 6 (IPv6) is the newest modification of the Internet Protocol (IP), the systems protocol that provides a recognition and place system for computer systems on systems and tracks visitors across the Online. IPv6 was developed by the Internet Engineering Task Force (IETF) to cope with the long-anticipated problem of IPv4 cope with fatigue.

IPv6 is developed to substitute IPv4, which still provides many online traffics as of 2013.As of Sept 2013, the amount of customers attaining Search engines services over IPv6 exceeded 2% for the first time.

Every system on the Online must be allocated an IP cope with in order to connect with other gadgets. With the ever-increasing number of new gadgets being linked with the Online, the need occurred for more details than IPv4 is able to provide. IPv6 uses a 128-bit cope with, enabling 2128, or roughly 3.4×10^{38} details, or more than 7.9×10^{28} times as many as IPv4, which uses 32-bit details. IPv4 allows only roughly 4.3 billion addresses. The two techniques are not developed to be interoperable, further complicating the conversion to IPv6.

IPv6 addresses are showed as eight categories of four hexadecimal numbers divided by colons, for example 2001:0db8:85a3:0042:1000:8a2e:0370:7334, but techniques of acronym of this full note are available.

The advantages and disadvantages of IPv6 are as follows:

Advantages:
*Provides more address with area (which is being required in bigger business scales-example Comcast)
*More highly effective online (128bit in comparison to IPv4's present 32 bit)
*Provides and overall bigger range internet-which again will be required in the future
*Address allowance is done by the product itself
*Assistance for protection using (IPSec) Internet Protocol Security

Disadvantages:
*It will be much more complicated to keep in mind IP address (compared to the details now)
*Developing a sleek conversion from IPv4 to IPv6
*IPv6 is not available to devices that run IPv4
*Any customer expenses in having to substitute an IPv4 machine
*A chance to turn over to IPv6

2.3 Routing:

Routing is the procedure of choosing best tracks in a network system along which to send system traffic. Routing is conducted for many kinds of systems, such as the telephone system (circuit switching), digital information systems (such as the Internet).

In bundle changing network systems, routing guides bundle sending (the transportation of rationally resolved system packages from their source toward their greatest destination) through advanced nodes. Intermediate nodes are typically system components gadgets such as routers, connects, gateways, fire walls, or changes. General-purpose computer systems can also forward packages and perform routing, though they are not specific components and are affected from restricted performance. The routing procedure usually guides sending on the basis of routing platforms which maintain a record of the tracks to various system locations. Thus, building routing platforms, which are organized in the router's memory, is very important for efficient routing.

Most routing methods use only one system path at a time. Multipath routing techniques allow the use of several other ways.

In the situation of overlapping/equal tracks, the following components are regarded to be able to choose which tracks get set up into the redirecting desk (sorted by priority):

Routing in a more filter feeling of the term is often compared with connecting in its supposition that system details are organized and that similar details indicate vicinity within the system. Structured details allow a single routing table admission to signify the path to a number of gadgets. In large systems, organized dealing with (routing, in the filter sense) outperforms unstructured dealing with (bridging). Routing has become the prominent form of dealing with on the Internet. Bridging is still commonly used within nearby surroundings.

Advantages of Routing:

*Prefix-Length: Where more time subnet covers are recommended (independent if it is within a redirecting method or over different redirecting protocol)

*Metric: Where a reduced metric/cost is recommended (only legitimate within one and the same redirecting protocol)

*Management distance: Where a reduced range is recommended (only legitimate between different redirecting protocols)

* Router forwards data based on router algorithms to other routers or hosts.

Disadvantages of Routing:
*Routing software decrypts the secured data, so its insecure period during which enemy, hacker can strike within the router.
*Routers need to be designed to allow inbound relationship to a certain computer.

2.3.1 Routing Information Protocol:
RIP (Routing Information Protocol) is a widely-used method for handling wireless router information within a self-contained system such as a company LAN (LAN) or a connected number of such LANs. RIP is categorized by the Internet Engineering Task Force (IETF) as one of several inner entrance methods (Interior Gateway Protocol).

Using RIP, an entrance variety (with a router) delivers its whole redirecting desk (which address all the other serves it knows about) to its nearest next door neighbor variety every half a minute. The next door neighbor variety in convert will successfully pass the details on to its next door neighbor and so on until all serves within the system have the same information of redirecting routes, a condition known as system unity. RIP uses a hop depend as a way to figure out system range. (Other methods use more innovative methods including moment as well.) Each variety with a wireless router in the system uses the redirecting desk details to figure out the next variety to path a bundle for a specified location.

RIP is regarded an effective remedy for small homogeneous networking systems. For bigger, more complex networking systems, RIP's transmitting of the whole redirecting desk every Half a minute may put a large amount of extra visitors in the networking system.

The significant substitute to RIP is the Open Shortest Path First Protocol (OSPF).

Advantages of Routing Information protocol:
   * Easy to configure and use

*Since it has been around so long time, it is well known to all and widely used.

Disadvantages of Routing Information protocol:
*Restricted to a hop depend of 15 after a bundle moves through 15 routers and still has another router to journey to, it will be removed.
*Does not assistance a variable-length subnet masking calculation (VLSM), which indicates that it delivers redirecting up-dates centered only on a fixed-length subnet masking calculation (FLSM) or tracks that drop on classful limitations. So RIP V1 will not perform with a system that has been sub netted beyond the regular /8, /16, /24 (255.0.0.0, 255.255.0.0, 255.255.255.0) or Category A, B, and C network system limitations.

* Converges gradually, especially on large networks
* Does not have information of the data transfer usage of a link
* Does not assistance several routes for the same route
* Redirecting up-dates can need important data transfer usage, as the whole routing desk is sent when a link's position changes
* Susceptible to routing loops

There are two older version of RIP they are given below:

RIP version 1: The exclusive specifications of RIP, described in RFC 1058, uses classful course-plotting. The frequent course-plotting up-dates do not carry subnet details; losing support for different length subnet includes variable length subnet masks (VLSM). This limitation makes it challenging to have different-sized subnets within of the same program classification. In other conditions, all subnets in a program classification must have the same size. There is also no support for Wi-Fi, creating RIP vulnerable to various attacks.

RIP version 2: Due to the inadequacies of the unique RIP requirements, RIP version2 (RIPv2) was designed in 1993 and last consistent in 1998. It involved the capability to bring subnet information, thus assisting Classless Inter-Domain Redirecting (CIDR). To sustain in reverse interface, the hop depend restrict of 15 stayed. RIPv2 has features to completely interoperate with the previously requirements if all Must Be Zero method areas in the RIPv1 information are effectively specified. Moreover, an interface change feature allows fine-grained interoperability improvements.

In an attempt to prevent needless fill on servers that do not get involved in routing, RIPv2 multicasts the whole routing desk to all nearby routers at the deal with 224.0.0.9, in contrast to RIPv1 which uses transmitted. Unicast dealing with is still permitted for special programs. (MD5) verification for RIP was presented in 1997. RIPv2 is conventional Internet Standard (which is RFC 2453).

Route labels were also included in RIP version 2. This performance allows for tracks to be recognized from inner tracks to exterior reassigned tracks from EGP methods.

Figure no 1: A structure of Routing Information Protocol

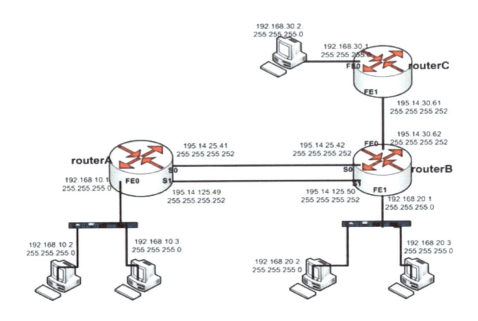

2.3.2 RIP next generation:

RIPng (RIP next generation), described in RFC 2080 is an expansion of RIPv2 for assistance of IPv6, the next generation internet protocol. RIP next generation (RIPng) is an internal gateway protocol (IGP) that uses distance-vector criteria to figure out the best path to a location, using the hop depends as the measurement. RIPng is a routing method that transactions routing details used to estimate tracks and is designed for IP edition 6 (IPv6)-based networks the primary variations between RIPv2 and RIPng are:

Advantages of RIP next generation:

*Support of IPv6 social media.
*While RIPv2 facilitates RIPv1 up-dates verification, RIPng does not. IPv6 routers were, at enough time, expected to use IPSec for verification.
 *RIPv2 allows linking irrelevant labels to tracks, RIPng does not;
 *RIPv2 encodes the next-hop into each path records; RIPng needs particular development of the next hope for a set of path records.
*RIPng delivers up-dates on UDP slot 521 using the multicast team FF02::9.
*It's a consistent protocol
* It's VLSM compliant
*Provides quick unity, and delivers activated up-dates when the system changes
 *Performs with overview routing - making it perfect for dial networks

Disadvantages of RIP next generation:
*Max hop count of 15, due to the 'count-to-infinity' weakness
*No concept of neighbors
*Exchanges entire table with all neighbors every 30 seconds (except in the case of a triggered update)

Figure 2: the structure of RIP Next Generation

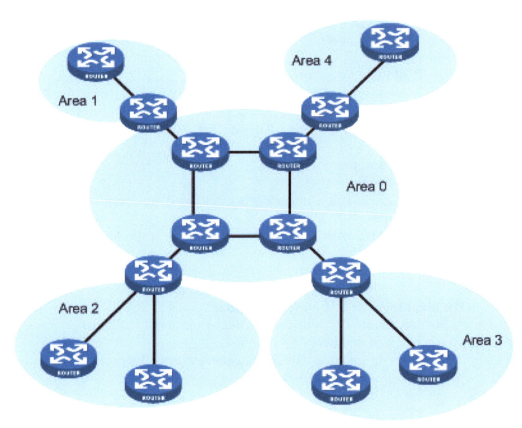

2.4 Switching:

Switching take up the same place in the system as locations. Compared with locations, switches analyze each bundle and process it accordingly rather than simply duplicating the indication to all slots. Switching map the Ethernet details of the nodes living on each system section and then allows only the necessary visitors to successfully go through the change. When a bundle is obtained by the switch, the switch investigates the location and resource components details and analyzes them to a desk of system sections and details. If the sections are the same, the bundle is decreased or "filtered"; if the sections are different, then the bundle is "forwarded" to the appropriate section. Furthermore, switches avoid bad or out of alignment packages from growing by not sending them.

Filtering packages and regenerating submitted packages allows changing technological innovation to divide a system into individual websites. The re-growth of packages allows for greater ranges and more nodes to be used in the complete networking system design, and considerably decreases the overall accident rates. In turned network, each section is an individual accident sector. This also allows for parallelism, significance up to one-half of the computer systems linked with a change can deliver information at the same time. In distributed networking systems all nodes live in a single distributed collision domain.

Easy to set up, most switches are self learning. They figure out the Ethernet details in use on each section, building a desk as packages are approved through the change. This "plug and play" factor makes switches an eye-catching substitute to locations.

Switches can web link different networking system types (such as Ethernet and Quick Ethernet) or networking systems of the same type. Many switches these days offer high-speed hyperlinks, like Quick Ethernet, which can be used to web link the switches together or to give included information transfer usages to important web servers that get a lot of visitors. A system consisting of a number of switches linked together via these fast uplinks is known as a "collapsed backbone" networking system.

Dedicating slots on switches to individual nodes is another way to rate access for crucial computer systems. Servers and professional users can take benefits of a complete section for one node, so some systems web link great traffics nodes to a devoted change slot.

Full duplex is another method to increase information transfer usages to devoted work stations or web servers. To use complete duplex, both system interface credit cards used in the server or work area and the change must assistance complete duplex function. Full duplex enhances the potential information bandwidth on that web link.

Advantages of switching:

Switching substitute locations in social media styles and they are more expensive. So why is the switching market increasing every year with huge figures sold? The cost of switches is

Decreasing precipitously, while locations are older technology with little cost decreases. This means that there is far less distinction between switch expenses and hub expenses than there used to be, and the gap is reducing.

Since switches are self learning, they are as simple to set up as a hub. Just connect them in and go. And they function on the same components part as a hub, so there are no method problems.

There are two reasons for switches being involved in system styles. First, a change smashes one system into many little systems so the range and repeater restrictions are re-booted. Second, this same segmentation isolates traffic and decreases crashes reducing system blockage. It is very simple to recognize the need for range and repeater expansion, and to comprehend this advantage of network system switching. But the second advantage, reducing system blockage, is hard to recognize and more complicated to comprehend the level by which switches will help performance. Since all switches add little latency setbacks to bundle handling, implementing switches needlessly can actually slowly down system performance. So the next area relates to the aspects impacting the effect of switching to congested networks.

Disadvantages of switching:

*Issue solitude: Issue solitude is easier with turned systems in that each pc is on its own cable. That generally becomes smaller the issue down to only the machine on a given switch port. In a turned environment, the pc that is causing the issue is generally the only pc that has a network system problem -- other computers can continue to operate on the network system without disruption.

* **Price:** One drawback of changing technological innovation is that it is more costly. Changes price more than locations, due to the complexness level and the functions that they provide. Hubs are generally foolish connection containers for network system cables, so their price is lower.

* **Support Costs:** Another drawback of turned system technological innovation is that it is more complicated. This implies that you have to have an individual who is qualified on the devices, and can keep the network system up and operating at its optimum. Such an individual can also fix system issues more easily than an inexperienced individual, but expenses more to implement.

2.5 Hot Standby Router Protocol:

Hot Standby Router Protocol (HSRP) is a routing protocol that allows variety computer systems on the Online to use several routers that act as only one exclusive router, keeping connection even if the first hop router is not available, because other routers are on "hot standby" - prepared to go. Designed on 'Cisco' routers operating the Internet Protocol (IP) over Ethernet, Fibers Distributed-Data Interface (FDDI), and local area network (LANs), HSRP provides automated router back-up. The protocol is completely suitable with Novell's Internetwork Bundle Return (IPX), AppleTalk, and Banyan VINES, and (in some configurations) with Xerox System Systems (XNS) and DECnet.

Developed by 'Cisco' and specified in IETF Demand for Feedback (RFC) 2281, HSRP guarantees that only one router (called the effective router) is sending packages on part of the exclusive router at any given time. A standby router is selected to be prepared to become the effective router, in the occasion that the current effective router is not able. HSRP describes a procedure used to figure out effective and standby routers by making reference to their IP details. Once these are identified, the failing of an effective router will not cause any important disruption of connection.

On any given LAN, there may be several, possibly the real, hot standby categories, each with only single Media Access Control (MAC) deal with and IP address; the IP deal with should the part of the main subnet, but must be different from any real or exclusive details assigned to any routers or serves on the network.

Hot Standby Router Protocol Load Sharing:
Router 1

```
track 1 interface Serial0/0/0.1 ip routing  ! Points
at the interface that needs to be Prioritized
interface FastEthernet0/0
 description interface to LAN
 ip address 10.10.10.1 255.255.255.0    ! Make sure
this IP is in the same subnet as your Virtual Gateway1
IP
 ip address 192.168.1.1 255.255.255.0 Secondary    !
Make sure this IP is in the same subnet as your
Virtual Gateway2 IP
 standby 1 ip 10.10.10.25                ! Virtual IP 1
(10.10.10.0 Network Takes Priority)
 standby 1 priority 105                  ! The Higher
the # The Higher the Priority
 standby 1 preempt                       ! Enables the
router with the highest priority to immediately become
the active router
 standby 1 track 1                       ! WAN
SUBINTERFACE
 standby 2 ip 192.168.1.25               ! Virtual IP 2
 standby 2 priority 100                  ! Lower
Priority = Backup Route
 standby 2 preempt                       ! Enables the
router with the highest priority to immediately become
the active router
 standby 2 track 1                       ! WAN
SUBINTERFACE
```

```
!
 Router bgp <ASN>
  network 10.10.10.0 mask 255.255.255.0   ! Broadcasts
Gateway1 out the WAN through BGP
  network 192.168.1.0 mask 255.255.255.0  ! Broadcasts
Gateway2 out the WAN through BGP
```

Router 2:

```
track 1 interface Serial0/0/0.1 ip routing  ! Points
at the interface that needs to be Prioritized
interface FastEthernet0/0
 description interface to LAN
 ip address 192.168.1.2 255.255.255.0     ! Make sure
this IP is in the same subnet as your Virtual Gateway2
IP
 ip address 10.10.10.2 255.255.255.0 Secondary    !
Make sure this IP is in the same subnet as your
Virtual Gateway1 IP
 standby 1 ip 10.10.10.25                ! Virtual IP 1
 standby 1 priority 100                  ! Lower
Priority = Backup Router
 standby 1 preempt                       ! Enables the
router with the highest priority to immediately become
the active router
 standby 1 track 1                       ! WAN
SUBINTERFACE
 standby 2 ip 192.168.1.25               ! Virtual IP 2
(192.168.1.0 Network Takes Priority)
 standby 2 priority 105                  ! The Higher
the # The Higher the Priority
 standby 2 preempt                       ! Enables the
router with the highest priority to immediately become
the active router
 standby 2 track 1                       ! WAN
SUBINTERFACE
!
 Router bgp <ASN>
  network 10.10.10.0 mask 255.255.255.0   ! Broadcasts
Gateway1 out the WAN through BGP
  network 192.168.1.0 mask 255.255.255.0  ! Broadcasts
Gateway2 out the WAN through BGP
```

Hot Standby Router Protocol Primary and Backup

Router 1

```
track 1 interface Serial0/0/0.1 ip routing  ! Points
at the interface that needs to be Prioritized
interface FastEthernet0/0
 description interface to LAN
 ip address x.x.x.x 255.255.255.0
 standby 1 ip <Gateway>                      ! Virtual IP
(IP Virtual)
 standby 1 priority 105                 ! Higher
Priority = Primary Router
 standby 1 preempt                           ! Enables the
router with the highest priority to immediately become
the active router
 standby 1 track 1                           ! WAN
SUBINTERFACE
!
 Router bgp <ASN>
  network <Gateway> mask 255.255.255.0  ! Broadcasts
Gateway out the WAN through BGP
```

Router 2

```
track 1 interface Serial0/0/0.1 ip routing  ! Points
at the interface that needs to be Prioritized
interface FastEthernet0/0
 description interface to LAN
 ip address x.x.x.x 255.255.255.0
 standby 1 ip <Gateway>                      ! Virtual IP
 standby 1 priority 100                      ! Lower
Priority = Backup Router
 standby 1 preempt                           ! Enables the
router with the highest priority to immediately become
the active router
 standby 1 track 1                           ! WAN
SUBINTERFACE
!
 Router bgp <ASN>
  network <Gateway> mask 255.255.255.0  ! Broadcasts
Gateway out the WAN through BGP
```

2.6 Graphical Network Simulator:

GNS3 is a free, GUI Network Simulator. It can be used to imitate complicated systems while being as close as possible from the way real systems perform, all of this without having devoted network components such as routers and changes.

GNS3 provides a user-friendly GUI to design and set up exclusive systems, it operates on traditional PC components and may be used on several operating-systems, such as Windows, Linux and Mac OS X.

Who can use this GUI Network Simulator: GNS3 will be used for program technicians, Network administrator, directors and individuals who are planning for certification like 'Cisco' CCNA, CCNP and CCIE and Juniper JNCIA, JNCIS and JNCIE. It can also be used to research functions or to examine options that need to be implemented later on actual gadgets.

GNS3 contains interesting functions, for example relationship of your exclusive program to actual ones or bundle catches using Wireshark. Also VirtualBox assistance is involved in GNS3 so that network , program administrator and technicians can take benefits of GNS3 to create laboratories, analyze program functions and research for Redhat (RHCE, RHCT) and Microsoft corporation (MCSE, MCSA) certification etc.

2.7 VMware Technology:

VMware is a virtualization and cloud computing application S/W company for x86-compatible computer systems. VMware, Inc. is a United States software company that provides cloud and virtualization application and services, being the first who handled to virtualize the x 86 structures. It was established in 1998 and centered in Palo Alto, California, USA. In 2004, it was obtained by EMC Corporation and now functions as a subsidiary company.

VMware's pc application operates on Microsoft corporation OS Microsoft windows, Linux system, and Mac OS X, while its business application hypervisors for web servers, VMware ESX and VMware ESXi, are bare-metal included hypervisors that run straight on server components without demanding an extra actual OS. VMware Inc. is an additional of EMC Corporation and has its head office in Palo Alto, California.

VMware virtualization is in accordance with the ESX/ESXi simple steel hypervisor, assisting exclusive devices. The phrase "VMware" is often used in referrals to particular VMware Inc. items such as VMware Workstation, VMware View, VMware Horizon Application Manager and VMware vCloud Director. and VMware vCloud Home.
VM, which appears for "Virtual Machine" (not to be puzzled with the wider phrase Virtual machine), is a widely-installed OS for IBM-compatible laptop or computer and web servers that can variety other operating-system in such a way that each OS acts as if it were set up on a self-contained laptop or computer with its own set of applications and components sources.

Advantages of VMware: VMware works by shifting all exclusive devices that run on an unsuccessful ESX server to another ESX server in the same failover group and restoring those VMs. A new function of VMHA allows server virtualization directors to observe VMs that run in a virtualized atmosphere for hosts' OS problems. If a visitor OS is not able, VMHA can even reboot that VM on another ESX server in the same high-availability group.
Not all catastrophe restoration needs include large information center-wide circumstances. In many cases, the physical components on a server can don't succeed, resulting in crucial company programs to be not available. VMHA can provide business a continual by quickly restoring VMs that run on an unsuccessful ESX server before you are able to get up out of bed and find out why you got a written text about a program failure.

Disadvantages of VMware:

Even though VMHA makes all your exclusive devices high-availability web servers, those hosts VMs still have to be restarted after they have shifted. And, VMHA performs on the supposition that either visitor the OS installed or the actual ESX Server damaged.

If you want a technological innovation that doesn't need a VM in the server group to be restarted, examine out VMware Mistake Patience.

VMware's Great Accessibility (VMHA) is provided in 5 of the 6 vSphere editions - Essentials Plus, Standard, Advanced, Enterprise and Enterprise Plus. Additionally VMware's vCenter is required.

2.8 Domain Name System:

The internet Domain Name System DNS converts online domain and host name to IP address. DNS instantly transforms the titles we type in our Web internet browser deal with bar to the IP address of web servers hosting those sites.

DNS utilizes an allocated data source to store this name and deal with information for all public hosts on the Online. DNS represents IP addresses do not change (are statically allocated rather than dynamically assigned).The DNS data source exists on a structure of special data source web servers. When customers like Web internet explorer issue demands including Online variety titles, a software called the DNS resolver (usually built into the networking system) first connections a DNS server to determine the server's IP address. If the DNS server does not contain the needed applying, it will convert and forward the demand to a different DNS server at the next advanced level in the structure. After possibly several sending and delegation information are sent within the DNS structure, the IP deal with for the given variety gradually comes at the resolver, that in convert finishes the demand over Internet Protocol.

DNS additionally contains assistance for caching demands and for redundancy. Most operating-system assistance settings of primary, additional, and tertiary DNS web servers, each of which can support initial demands from customers. Internet Service Providers (ISPs) maintain their own DNS web servers and use DHCP to instantly set up customers, reducing most home users of the pressure of DNS settings.

Advantages of DNS: DNS web servers allow conventional online surfers to use online sources without having to remember slot figures and IP addresses. Even identical services, such as different places of the website, may be organized at different IP addresses for protection reasons. This allows customers to remember simple URL details in contrast to complicated, nonnutritive details of IP address and slot figures. This also allows personal web servers made by home customers to be easily available yet somewhat guarded from having their IP addresses with openly known.

Disadvantages of DNS: On the other hand, using DNS-based redirection results in a few complications. The first of them is due to the fact that DNS issues bring no information about the consumer that activated the name quality.

All that the service-side DNS server knows is the system address of the DNS server that requests about the support place.

Therefore, we have to believe that customers always use a DNS Therefore, we have to believe that customers always use a DNS server that is near to them, and estimated a customer's place to that of its DNS server. Whether we consider it to be a disadvantage or not relies on the precision we want to accomplish.
Studies display that 64% of customers are in the same system as their DNS web servers. Thus, as long as we do not need tight per client redirection, the place of the consumer DNS server approximates the consumer well enough

2.9 File Transfer Protocol:

File Transfer Protocol (FTP) is a standard IP address for transferring information between two computers on the Online. Like the Hypertext Transfer Protocol (HTTP), which exchanges displayable Web pages and related information, and the Simple Mail Transfer Protocol (SMTP), which exchanges e-mail, FTP is an application protocol that uses the Web's TCP/IP methods. FTP is widely used to transfer Web page information from their creator to the pc that acts as their server for everyone on the Online. It's also widely used to download programs and other information to your pc from other servers. FTP allows you to exchange information files between two computer systems on the Online. FTP is an easy system method based on Internet Protocol and also a term used.

When making reference to the process of duplicating information files when using FTP technology.

To exchange information files with FTP, you use a system often known as the consumer. An FTP customer system triggers a connection to a distant computer operating FTP server software.

After the connection is recognized, the consumer can choose to deliver and/or get duplicates of information files, singly or in categories. To get connected to an FTP server, a user needs addresses as set by the manager of the server. Many public FTP records follow a special conference for that allows a login name of "anonymous."

Simple FTP customers are involved with most system operating-system, but most of these customers (such as FTP.EXE on Windows) assistance a relatively unfavorable command-line customer interface. Many substitute third-party FTP user have been designed that assistance graphic user interfaces (GUIs) and additional comfort features. In any FTP customer interface, customers recognize the FTP server either by its IP address with (such as 192.168.0.1) or by its variety name (such as ftp.about.com).

FTP facilitates two ways of information transfer: simply written text (ASCII), and binary. You set the method in the FTP user. A common mistake when using FTP is trying to exchange a binary information file (such as a system, programs or music file) while in written text method, resulting in the moved information file to be useless.

Advantages of FTP:

*FTP is the quick and effective way of transferring bulks of information across the World Wide Web.

* It has an automated back-up .Whenever you modify your data files in your regional program you can upgrade the same by duplicating it to the variety program in your website. So in situations where your website has damaged and all the information is missing you have a duplicate of it in your own regional program. It also performs the other way circular.

* FTP gives you management over exchange. That is, you can select the method in which the information is moved over the system. The information can be moved either in the ASCII method (for written text files) or in the Binary mode (for executables or compacted files).

*You can perform with the World Wide Web directories on the distant techniques, remove or re-label the distant data files while shifting information between 2 serves.

*While using FTP, resources like macros can also be used to create it more effective and simpler.

Disadvantages of FTP:
*FTP was not developed to be a protected method.

*FTP causes the following strikes during the exchange of information.

a. Bounce Attacks

b.Spoof Attacks

c.BruteForce Attacks

d.Packet Sniffing

e.Username protection

f. Port sealing

*Security of information is not proper in FTP.

2.10 Internet Information Services:

IIS (Internet Information Server) is a group of online web servers (including a Web or HTTP server and a File Transfer Protocol server) with additional abilities for Microsoft Windows NT and Microsoft windows 2000 Server operating-system. IIS is Microsoft windows admission to contend in the online server market that is also resolved by Apache, Sun Microsystems, O'Reilly, and others. With IIS, Microsoft Corporation has a set of programs for building and providing websites, an internet search engine, and support for writing Web-based programs that accessibility data source. Microsoft corporation points out that IIS are firmly incorporated with the Microsoft Windows NT and 2000 Servers in various ways, leading to faster Website providing.

A common company that purchases IIS can create WebPages for websites using Microsoft windows Front Web page product (with its WYSIWYG user interface). Web designers can use Microsoft windows Active Server Web page (ASP) technology, which means that programs - such as ActiveX manages - can be imbedded in Websites that change the content sent back to customers. Developers can also write programs that narrow demands and get the correct Websites for different customers by using Microsoft windows Online Server Application Program User interface (ISAPI) interface. ASPs and ISAPI programs run more efficiently than common gateway interface (CGI) and server-side include (SSI) programs, two current technologies. (However, there are similar connections on other systems.)

Microsoft contains special abilities for server directors developed to entice Internet service suppliers (ISPs). It has a single window (or "console") from which all services and customers can be applied it's developed to be easy to add elements as snap-ins that you didn't originally set up. The management windows can be personalized for accessibility by individual customers.

Microsoft has been belittled for IIS's vulnerability to Trojan strikes such as Code Red and Nimda.

Advantages of IIS:

* Inexpensive of implementation per customer: End users of an IIS program can run the program using only a browser; no special software needs to be installed on their computers for the program to perform.

*A familiar growth atmosphere and design: You can make use of your knowledge of Visible Primary by using the Visible Primary programming atmosphere and standard, collected Visible Primary rule. In addition, you can add classes, segments, or any Visible Primary ActiveX component to your project.

*Accessibility a broad viewer: IIS programs perform with an extensive range of browsers and operating-system, so you can quickly reach extensive viewers.

*An item design that gives you accessibility to resources of the Online Details Server: The Active Server Pages structure provides an item design that allows you to directly operate the things at the core of IIS. This allows you to retrieve information from an internet browser, send information to it, and perform complex functions on the contents of a Web page. To learn more about the item design, see "The Object Model for IIS Applications."

*Recyclable components: Once you have created a web class, you can quickly access in another web class.

*Separation of rule and HTML: Unlike scripting, your rule is not embedded in the HTML document, so you can separate the procedure of developing the application's user interface from writing, testing, and debugging its rule.

*Condition control across multiple communications with the consumer: You can manage state using things or a database, or you can shuttle state between the consumer and the server.

> ***Structured processing:** You do not have to make the HTML design information your program sends to the World Wide Web browser, if you do not want to. In Visible Primary Online database integration, the procedure of developing your user interface is divided from the procedure of developing and coding your program. You can have a designer make the design information you want to use.

Disadvantages of IIS:

*Individual Information: If you use the Online, your private details such as your name, address   etc. can be utilized by other people. If you use a bank cards to buy online, then your bank cards details can also be 'stolen' which could be similar to providing someone an empty check.

*Pornography: This is a very serious problem concerning the Online, especially when it comes to youngsters. There are a large number of adult websites on the Online that can be quickly discovered and can be a hindrance to allowing kids use the Online.

*Spamming: This represents delivering unwanted e-mails in large, which provide no objective and needlessly block up the whole system.

*Piracy: By using IIS many bad people pirate much important information.

2.11 Ipv4 and Ipv6 Solution:

Ipv4 and Ipv6 transition mechanisms: IPv6 is developed as a transformative update to the IPv4 and will, actually, exist together with the mature edition for some time. The incorporation and coexistence of IPv4 and IPv6 need to be well described and organized. To create the conversion to IPv6 simpler, the Internet Engineering Task Force (IETF) has set up a perform team known as Next Generation Transition or shortly NGTrans, which their task is to specify systems for assisting interoperability between IPv4 and IPv6. This has been the focus of the IETF NGTrans for several decades. NGTrans has recognized the conversion systems and released several requirements that explain the conversion mechanisms for IPv6 serves and routers. These mechanisms are intensely used for the conversion from the traditional IPv4-based Online to an IPv6-based Online. The conversion systems usually come in one of three following forms:

IPv6/IPv4 Dual Stack Approach: The first strategy and the most uncomplicated way to present IPv6-capable nodes is a dual stack approach, where this strategy needs serves and routers to apply both IPv4 and IPv6 protocols. In this technique a system node sets up both IPv4 and IPv6stacks in similar. This allows systems to support bothIPv4 and IPv6 solutions and programs during the transition interval in which IPv6 solutions appear and IPv6 applications become available.

When interacting with IPv6 nodes, they use IPv6 and when communicating with IPv4 nodes, they revert to IPv4. These nodes are known as IPv4 suitable IPv6 details, these are addressed s where the first 96 pieces of the deal with are zeroes and the last 32 pieces types a real IPv4 deal with .Dual-stack is required when an IPv6 system want to communicate with a local IPv4 serves and programs. The serves and programs in local IPv6 can communicate with the serves and program that used the same protocol. This strategy allows IPv4 and IPv6 program to coexist in a dual IP part redirecting central source. All routers or a concoction of them in the system need to be improved to be with IPv4 interaction using the dual stack IPv4 stack collection and IPv6 interaction using the IPv6 stack.

Tunneling: A substitute to the dual-stack approach is known as tunneling, also mentioned in RFC 2893 and can be used to get over the disadvantage in dual-stack approach. IPv6 tunneling is a strategy for developing a "virtual link" between two IPv6 nodes for transferring information packages as payloads of IPv6 packages. Different from dual-stack approach, tunneling encapsulates whole IPv6 datagram and places in the information area of an IPv4 datagram. The IPv4 packet will travel within the IPv4 system and upon arrival at the IPv6 system the location node is located in the IPv4 headlines will be removed and the encapsulated IPv6 bundle will be sent to its destination.

Translation Mechanism: The last strategy in uses a Translation mechanism. Translation is necessary when an IPv6 only variety has to connect with an IPv4 variety. At least, the IP header has to be converted but the interpretation will be more complicated if the program procedures IP details. In reality such translation gets most of the issues of IPv4 System Deal with Linguists (NAT). ALGs (Application-Level Gateways) are needed to convert embedded IP addresses; recomputed checksums example SIIT (Stateless IP/ICMP Translation) and NAT-PT (Network Deal with Translation Method Translation) are the associated translation methods.

2.12 Ipv4 and Ipv6 Implementation:

Implementation of IPv6 and IPv4 is growing across the world and system professionals are put the main attraction as this new method is added to their company's systems and network facilities. The detail description of IPv6 and IPv4 Implementation given below:

- Native Implementation

- Dual Stack Implementation

- IPv6 Tunneling

- IPv6 Only to IPv4 Only Translation

Native Implementation: The first execution method is to set up IPv6 in local settings. This setting configures all serves and routers to utilize IPv6 only and not together with IPv4.

Native execution boundaries the network to only IPv6 interaction to other systems and would require interpretation to interface other IPv4 systems.

Dual Stack Implementation: The second and most popular execution is dual stack. Dual stack execution allows IPv4 and IPv6 address to be available on the same physical and/or sensible interface. This execution is also the most convenient to apply in an atmosphere that already is recognized.

The primary issues for the double collection execution are in application and components. Hardware must be analyzed in the system facilities to see if there is proper storage for path platforms and the change sending platforms to deal with IPv6 tracks and packages. Software on the system facilities must support IPv6 settings and redirecting methods, while operating-system on the variety side must also be IPv6 capable.

IPv6 Tunneling: The next execution available for IPv6 is tunneling. Tunneling is used to link two local IPv6 implementations over a current IPv4 only system, which is generally seen as a WAN system.

Edge routers for each IPv6 execution are linked with the IPv4 system and a canal is designed between them. IPv6 unique headers and payloads are not customized in the canal, but instead an IPv4 headlines is placed at the front part of the IPv6 headlines for transmitting over the IPv4 system and then removed off on the other part.

IPv6 Only to IPv4 Only Translation: IPv6 only to IPv4 only translation is the last execution technique we will analyze. Why would we need this? Well, IPv6 nodes may need connections with IPv4 only nodes for certain solutions such as: email or web solutions.

There are several methods to achieve interpretation. The most generally technique used is Program Application Level Gateways (ALG), which runs on the server that act as proxies to solutions that may be other IPv6 or IPv4 nodes.

Chapter 3: Analysis

3.1 Methodology:

In the methodology section we want to show the method and objective of the analysis. For this reason we have analyzed the Dual Stack IPv4/IPv6 Performance Verification.

IPv4 and IPv6 hosts are required to available together for a significant time during the stable migration from IPv4 to IPv6, and the growth of conversion techniques, resources, and systems has been part of the IPv6 technological innovation since its beginning. From a examining viewpoint, this means that a primary dual-stack IPv4/IPv6 performance analyze should be regarded as a first step in developing a guideline not only for all upcoming IPv6 assessments but also as a way to comprehend any performance variations that may are available in the product when sending IPv4 traffic compared to IPv6 traffic.IPv4 and IPv6 serves are required to are available together for a significant time during the stable migration from IPv4 to IPv6, and the growth of conversion techniques, resources, and systems has been part of the IPv6 technological innovation since its beginning. From a examining viewpoint, this means that a primary dual-stack IPv4/IPv6 performance analyze should be regarded as a first step in developing a guideline not only for all upcoming IPv6 assessments but also as a way to comprehend any performance variations that may are available in the product when sending IPv4 traffic compared to IPv6 traffic.

3.2 Requirement collection process:
The required collection process for this analyze include:
• IPv4 and IPv6 details designed on the analyze slots running the Performance Endpoints to make two sets – Couple 1 for IPv4 and Couple 2 for IPv6
• IxChariot program – High Performance Throughput
• Network Protocol – TCP and TCP IPv6 respectively
• Run Option was set to a fixed length of one minute

3.3 Requirement collection protocols:

For this analysis we have required Network Protocol – TCP and TCP IPv6 respectively .Because TCP (Transmission Control Protocol) is a set of guidelines (protocol) used along with the Internet Protocol (IP) to deliver information in the form of concept models between computer systems over the Online. While IP manages managing the actual distribution of the information, TCP manages tracking the individual models of information (called packets) that a concept is separated into for effective routing through the Online. As we have analyzed Dual Stack IPv4/IPv6 Performance Verification so we have used TCP IPv6. It is the upgrade form TCP and necessary for this sort of analysis.

3.4 Requirement Analysis:

The main requirement of our analysis is to figure out and define any throughput variations that may available in the network system and particular Device under Test (DUT) when sending IPv4 and IPv6 traffic. This is important since many gadgets provide hardware-based speeding for IPv4; however, they either do not provide this choice for IPv6 or provide it only with the decreased performance.

3.5 Evaluation of Requirement:

Several NIC cards can be used to coordinate slots on the DUT. For only one ingress/egress slot couple, two sets are described (one for each IP address), and then implemented with run choices set to a fixed time.

Test Execution (Endpoint 1 to Endpoint 2)

Group/Pair	Endpoint 1	Endpoint 2	Network Protocol	Service Quality	Script/Stream Name
All Pairs					
Pair 1	172.21.4.4	172.22.4.4	TCP		High_Performance_Throughput.scr
Pair 2	2000:21::4	2000:22::4	TCP-IPv6		High_Performance_Throughput.scr

Throughput

Group/ Pair	Average (Mbps)	Minimum (Mbps)	Maximum (Mbps)	Throughput 95% Confidence Interval	Measured Time (secs)
All Pairs	265.158	19.935	265.781		
Pair 1	246.943	238.095	265.781	0.547	59.285
Pair 2	20.693	19.935	21.511	0.252	57.991
Totals:	265.158	19.935	265.781		

Figure 3: Baseline IPv4/IPv6 throughput performance test results through a Layer 3 switch

3.6 Requirement of Proposed Solution:

The requirement of the proposed solution is given as follows:

IxChariot reveals the throughput outcomes in several different methods (e.g., max, min, average), as well as showing outcomes as datagram statics, such as Bytes Sent and Obtained by E1. As can be seen in the clip from the IxChariot HTML review above, couple 1 (i.e., IPv4) reveals considerably better performance than couple 2 (i.e., IPv6), thus showing that the DUT provides better throughput for IPv4 than for IPv6 traffic.

Note: IxChariot actions the throughput associated with bundle payload, neglecting headers. This measurement is generally known as "Goodput" in RFC 2647.

Chapter 4: Design

4.1 Design Overview:

In the design chapter we have to design IPv6/IPv4 Addressing with NDRA and DHCPv6 Prefix Delegation network structure. The overview of this design is given below:

DHCPv6 prefix delegation to improve the delegation of IPv6 prefixes to the CPE. With prefix delegation, an assigning router (the BNG) associates IPv6 prefixes to an inquiring wireless router (the CPE). The inquiring wireless router then uses the prefixes to assign global IP details to the gadgets on the prospective subscriber LAN. The inquiring wireless router can also assign subnet details to subnets on the LAN.DHCPv6 prefix delegation is useful when the assigning router does not have information about the topology of the network systems in which the inquiring router is situated. In such cases, the assigning router needs only the identification of the inquiring wireless router to choose a prefix for delegation.

DHCPv6 prefix delegation changes the need for NAT in an IPv6 network.

4.2 Interaction design:

This design uses NDRA and DHCPv6 prefix delegation in your prospective subscriber accessibility network are as follows:

• The accessibility network in PPPoE.
• NDRA is used to allocate an international IPv6 address with on the WAN web link. The prefixes used in router ads come from a regional share that is specified using AAA RADIUS.
• DHCPv6 prefix delegation is used for prospective subscriber LAN dealing with. It uses a delegated prefix from a regional share that is specified using AAA RADIUS.
• DHCPv4 is used for prospective subscriber LAN addressing.
• DHCPv6 prospective subscriber classes are padded over an actual PPPoE prospective subscriber period.

4.3 Data Design:

This design uses NDRA and DHCPv6 prefix delegation in your Subscriber accessibility system as follows:

• NDRA addressing is used to supply an international IPv6 deal with on the WAN web link. IPv6 prefixes for NDRA come from a regional share or AAA RADIUS.

• DHCPv6 prefix delegation is used for variety network addresses. The assigned prefix can come from a regional share or from AAA RADIUS. The CPE uses the assigned prefix for subscriber addresses. The CPE can use NDRA or DHCPv6 to spend IPv6 addresses on the LAN.

4.4 Interface Design:
The interface design of the Subscriber Access Network with NDRA and DHCPv6 Prefix
Delegations are as follows:

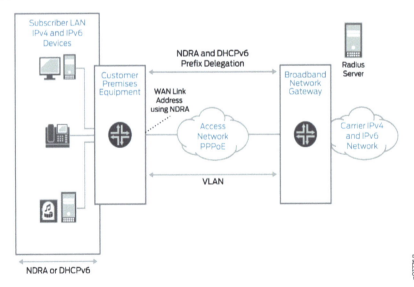

Figure 4: Subscriber Access Network with NDRA and DHCPv6 Prefix Delegation

Chapter 5: Testing and Implantation

5.1 Testing Strategy:

In our analysis chapter we already analyzed Dual Stack IPv4/IPv6 Performance Verification. Now we will show the output of the analysis in practical way by doing a test. The objective and strategy of our test is given below:

With IPv4 address space reducing by the second and the booming growth of the number of mobile computers, IPv6 has already been implemented and implemented by government departments, companies and businesses. IPv6 device improvements, from pc and application web servers, to social media products such as routers, switches, and security devices, have also increased the roll-out of IPv6 based network systems and services.

To get to know the high anticipations of the IPv6 system and support quality, and deal with the reality of dual stack IPv4/IPv6 traffic, companies are looking for an efficient, genuine and scalable device to evaluate the effect of dual stack traffic. Their ability to evaluate the performance, security and balance of any system managing IPv4/IPv6 visitors will straight determine if the release of any IPv6 based system and support is successful.

5.2 Test Plans:

As you have study here lately, Breaking Point has taken on the difficulties of IPv6 in our webcast and methodology. Both of these are excellent sources and we would motivate everyone to obtain the IPv6 Resiliency Methodology. But we desired to take enough time we have in this publish providing you a fast business presentation of how to quickly and effectively to set up a fast dual-stack IPv4/IPv6 analyze to evaluate against an IPv6 able social media factor and/or facilities.

Figure 1 below demonstrates the installation for an easy dual-stack IPv4/IPv6 simulator. We will make use of the Breaking Point Surprise CTM to simultaneously produce both IPv4 and IPv6 centered program traffic operating through the product under analyze (DUT) to examine whether it can manage both IPv4 and IPv6 traffic in as precise and scalable way as it does when working with IPv4 only traffic.

Figure 5: Dual-Stack IPV4/IPv6 Test Bed

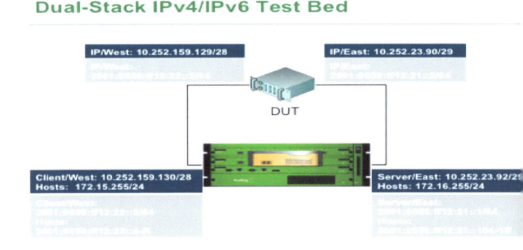

Just like giving both IPv4 and IPv6 addresses to a real variety, on the Breaking Point Strom CTM, you can spend both IPv4 and IPv6 deal with sections on only one interface at the same time to replicate several serves during the analyze run.

Let us start with interface 1 which symbolizes the consumer side. Here, we make two separate IPv4 and IPv6 deal with websites for this objective. As proven in Determine 2 below, under the IPv6 sector, we will spend an international unicastv6 address area (starting with 2001 ::) for this simulator.

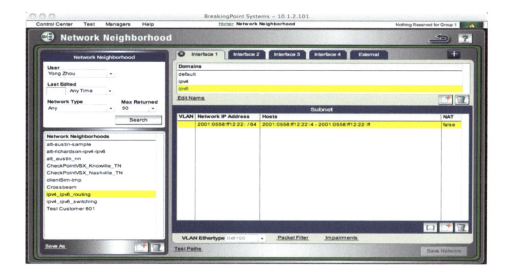

Figure 6: Testing Software Interface

Next, we do it again the identical actions for the Network Neighborhood installation on interface 2, which is the server part. Please bear in mind that to prevent a prospective system problem make sure that there is no the actual of the lower 64-bit of the IPv6 address with allowance on interface 1 and interface 2. This is due to devices providers only using the hashing of the reduced 64-bit deal with (instead of the complete 128-bit v6 address) when it comes to the v6 visitors sending. If one circulation keeping the same reduced 64-bit of the resource and location deal with (even though their greater 64-bit network details are different), the product will fall the bundle due to the identical source/destination deal with because of its reduced 64-bit hashing execution.

As proven in Determine 3 below, we will set up the real program traffic emulation for the analyze. This can be done via the Breaking Point Storm's Application Simulation (AppSim) element. For this dual-stack IPv4/IPv6 analyze, we need two AppSim elements, one for the IPv4 centered traffic and one for the IPv6 centered traffic.

Figure 7: Analysis of the IPv4/ IPv6 dual stack

For the IPv4 based application simulation, go to the AppSim interface setting and select the IPv4 domain of interface 1 as client and interface 2 as the server. Similarly, for the IPv6 based AppSim, please go to the AppSim interface setting and select the IPv6 domain of interface 1 and interface 2 as the client and server side.

5.3 Test Results (with Justification):

The result of the test with justification is as follows:
Besides the AppSim parameter configurations you may already know about within the Breaking Point Strom CTM, We suggest you also modify the TCP MSS dimension. As we know, the IPv6 deal with is 128-bit lengthy, as opposed to 32-bit lengthy IPv4 deal with. Therefore, the IPv6 centered IP headlines (refer to RFC2460 for details) is 40-Bytes lengthy as opposed to 20-Byte IPv4 headlines. To create sure that the analyze will not cause too many needless v6 bundle fragmentations, which affects the efficiency of the IPv6 traffics managed by the product, set the TCP MSS dimension to 1440 bytes. This will prevent the bundle fragmentation with the standard 1500 bytes MTU dimension both the product and the Breaking Point Strome CTM.

Figure 8: Test Result of the IPv4/ IPv6

Dual stack

Moreover, we should progressively add the IPv6 based traffics quantity to find the ability of the product as it manages the dual stack IPv4/IPv6 traffics at the same time. From our beginning analyze results, when it comes to the performance and scalability of the managing of IPv6 traffics, some gadgets could not coordinate the same standard it maintains for managing IPv4 only traffics.

1. Network Neighborhood Setup

2. Application Simulator Components Setup

5.4 Implementation Plan:
Beyond this simple but effective dual stack IPv4/IPv6 simulator, Breaking Point has offered an
In-depth technique, which reveals how to make more complicated assessments to be able to measure:
The capability of a network system to deliver IPv6 traffic
 *The capability of the device to deliver both IPv4 and IPv6 traffic
*The impact of deformed packages that is present on the present networks
*The impact of security risks on overall performance
*The impact make more secured network
*The impact changes the performance of both IPv4/IPv6.

This test and our technique, along with the Breaking Point Strom CTM, will have you ready for the onset trend of IPv6 traffics.

Chapter 6: Conclusion

6.1 Evaluation Review:

In this project we have shown IPv4 and IPv6 Technology and Implementation .We also discuss about the some feature of IPv4 and IPv6 and their advantages and disadvantages .Besides the IPv4 and IPv6 Technology we have also discussed about the various types of networking and internet technology and their advantages and disadvantages in our Lecture Review chapter their names are given below:

2.3 Routing
2.3.1 Routing Information Protocol
2.3.2 RIP next generation
2.4 Switching
2.5 Hot Standby Router Protocol
2.6 Graphical Network Simulator
2.7 VMware Technology
2.8 Domain Name System
2.9 File Transfer Protocol

In chapter three, four and five we have shown analysis, network design and a complete test with a perfect result. This all sort of things proof that our project is successful.

6.2 Evaluation of the Project Outcomes:

The outcome of the project is very much important for any types of project .In this project we have clearly shown the result and outcomes of our project. At first we have discussed about our Dual Stack IPv4/IPv6 Performance Verification test in our Analysis chapter. In this part we have shown the entire necessary requirement for the test and the possible outcome of the test. And the Test and Implementation chapter we have done a test with test plan, test result and implementation plan. We have got perfect result in our Dual Stack IPv4/IPv6 Performance Verification test. We have also discussed about the implementations of our test result in this Test and Implementation chapter.

So this sort of things shows and proof that our Evaluation of Project Outcomes is quite successful.

6.3 Evaluation of Project the Deliverables:

The project deliverables are discussed as follows:

After a lengthy time of examining, IPv6 is lastly becoming approved by the online world. It is apparent to say that two decades young method is providing enhancements into contemporary IP system through its new features and advantages. But, shifting straight from IPv4 to IPv6 is not a practical way because IPv4 and IPv6 are two absolutely individual methods, even though IPv6 was developed more as a progress and enhancement from IPv4. Conversion systems to allow the coexistence of IPv4 and IPv6 have to be consistent. The integration and coexistence of IPv4 and IPv6 need to be well described and organized and this has been the concentrate of the IETF NGtans for several decades. NGtans has identified the transition systems and released several specifications that explain the transition systems for IPv6 serves and routers. These systems are heavily used for the transition from the traditional IPv4-based Internet to an IPv6-based Internet.

6.4 Evaluation of the Project Practices:

These days, plenty of performs and studies have been done on IPv6/IPv4 and its relevant problems, and there is still a long way to go. To tests and comprehend the part which IPv6/IPv4 will perform later on, it is necessary for us to create arms on encounter with the IPv6 technology. Through our effort in developing an IPv6/IPv4 test-bed in UUM have allow us to create this skills and become officially qualified with IPv6 technological innovation in an academic atmosphere. The effort to develop this test-bed can improve our information towards the IPv4 to IPv6 transition and migration. We have also been able to discover the primary of IPv6 technological innovation and produce many studies such as the execution of transition systems, new IPv6/IPv4 program examining, IPv6/IPv4 performance analysis, cellular IPv6/IPv4 technology, advantages, disadvantages of the technology and many more. It also provided us the opportunity to analyze and comprehend the IPv6/IPv4 technological innovation before any actual execution time comes. The discovering of this analysis could be used to other business establishing which plans apply IPv6/IPv4 in their system and their network.

At last we can say that, our project and the test result is helpful for the future research and the implementation of IPv4 and IPv6 technology. We hope this book is helpful for expanding the future research work of the IPv4 and IPv6 technology

References and Citation

➢ Cisco System, The ABCs of IP version 6, Technical Report. Cisco IOS Learning Services, Cisco System. Available at http://www.cisco.com/warp/public/732/abc/docs/abcIPv6.pdf, 2002.

➢ Kessler, G.C., IPv6: The next generation Internet protocol. Handbook on Local Area Networks, Auerbach, 1997. Cisco System, IPv6 at a Glance. Courtesy of Cisco Enterprise Marketing, Cisco System, Inc. 2004.

➢ Awad-Murshed, G.A. and Komosny, D., Comparison of IPv4 and IPv6, Brno University of Technology, Brno, Czech Republic, 2004.

➢ Raicu, I., An empirical analysis of Internet Protocol version 6 (IPv6), Master Thesis, Wayne State University, 2002.

➢ ENST-Bretagne, DSTM V2.0Beta for FreeBSD and Linux, Ecole Nationale Superieure de Telecommunications de Bretagne, France. 2003b.

➢ S. Lawson. "Update: ICANN assigns its last IPv4 Addresses," Computerworld, February03,2011.

http://www.computerworld.com/s/article/9207961/Update_ICANN_assigns_its_last_IPv4_addresses

➢ J. Brzozowski,"IPv6 Business Case Review: Strategy and Migration," 6UK Launch Event - Comcast, 11 November 2010.

➢ "6rd Configuration Instructions," Comcast, 30 Jun., 2011

➢ Y. L. Lee, " Dual-Stack Lite - Analyzing how to deliver Internet applications over DS-Lite," NANOG 50, 06 Oct., 2010

➢ "IPv6 Large Scale Network Address Translation," *Broadband Internet Tech. Advisory Group*, Mar. 2012.

➢ M. Bagnulo and F. Baker, "IPv4/IPv6 Co-existence and Transition: Requirements for Solutions," IETF 71. Mar. 2008.

➢ T. Rooney, "Service Provider IPv6 Deployment Strategies," BT Diamond IP, 2011.

➢ M. Ciglarc et al. "Practical Evaluation of Stateful NAT4/DNS64 Translation," *Advances in Elect. And Comput. Eng.*, vol. 11, no. 3, pp. 49-55, 2011.

Websites List:

➢ http://www.cisco.com/en/US/prod/collateral/iosswrel/ps6537/ps6553/white_paper_c11-676278.html

➢ http://www.cs.washington.edu/research/networking/napt/reports/usenix98/

➢ http://www.trainsignal.com/blog/ipv6-implementation

➢ http://www.domainnews.com/en/permanent-adoption-of-ipv6-moves-step-closer-with-world-ipv6-launch.html

➢ http://mashable.com/category/ipv4/

➢ http://wiki.answers.com/

➢ http://www.computerworld.com/s/article/9207961/Update_ICANN_assigns_its_last_IPv4_addresses

➢ http://www.ehow.com/

About the Author

Ghazi Mokammel Hossain is a professional article, research paper and creative writer. He has written many articles, research papers, and creative article. The author lives in Dhaka, Bangladesh. He was born in 31 December 1993. The name of his father is Ghazi Mozammel Hossain and his mother name is Syeda Taskin Ara. He has passed his S.S.C exam from Narinda Govt. High School, Dhaka under Dhaka Board in 2008 and passed his H.S.C exam from Ideal Commerce College, Dhaka under Dhaka Board in 2010. Now he is studying in BBA (Honors) 3rd year in Victoria University Bangladesh. He has also completed Computer Science and Engineering certificate course in 2011. Playing football, Cricket, PC games, Reading book, research paper, cycling and mountain climbing are his favorite hobbies.

The End

www.ingramcontent.com/pod-product-compliance
Lightning Source LLC
Chambersburg PA
CBHW041145050326
40689CB00001B/494